Arduino For Beginners

Beginners guide on How To Learn Arduino Advanced Methods and Strategies

By

Robert Campbell

Contents

Introduction

Every day, everyone makes use of technology. Most individuals delegate programming to experts because they believe electronics and coding are tough and complex; they may be enjoyable and interesting pursuits. Designers, artists, students, and hobbyists learn how to make objects that glow, move, and react to animals, people, plants, or the world, thanks to Arduino. Thousands of projects have utilized Arduino as the "brain" throughout the years, each more inventive than the previous. A global community of creators has rallied around this free source platform, transforming personal computing into personal fabrication and helping to a different era of participation, collaboration, and sharing. Arduino is a simple and open platform. You can make learning to use digital technologies easy and accessible if you start with that premise. Electronics and code have suddenly become artistic instruments that everyone can use, similar to paintbrushes and paint. This book takes you through the fundamentals in a hands-on manner, with creative projects that you create as you learn. Once you've learned the fundamentals, you'll be able to employ various circuits and software to construct something beautiful and make someone happy with your invention.

This book will teach you about the Arduino programming language, its applications, and how it works.

- The Arduino Board's Description

- Installation of an Arduino

- The Arduino Program's Structure

- Arduino's Data Types

- Arduino Variables & Constants

- Programmers for Arduino

- Arduino Control Statements

- Arduino's Loops

- Arduino's Advantages

- Arduino's Strings

- Arduino String Object

- Arduino's Arrays

Chapter-1 Arduino Overview

Arduino Uno is an open electronics platform that uses simple hardware and software to make it easy to use. Arduino boards can take inputs - such as light from any finger on a button, a sensor, a social media message - and convert them to outputs - such as switching on an LED, triggering a motor, or posting anything online. By providing a sequence of commands to the board's microcontroller. The Arduino software program (centered on wiring), as well as the Arduino Interface (IDE) (based on Processing), are used to do this.

Thousands of projects have used Arduino throughout the years, ranging from simple household items to complicated scientific apparatus. This open-source platform has united an international society of makers - students, programmers, artists, amateurs, and professionals - whose contributions have added to an enormous quantity of accessible information that may greatly benefit beginners and specialists alike.

Arduino was created at the "Ivrea Interaction Design Institute" as a simple tool for rapid prototyping intended for students with no previous experience with electronics or programming. As soon as it gained a larger following, the Arduino board began to evolve to meet new requirements and problems, evolving from basic 8-bit boards to solutions for IoT, 3D printing, wearables, and embedded settings.

1.1 Why Arduino?

Arduino has been utilized in millions of projects and applications because of its convenient user interface. Beginners will find the Arduino software simple to use, while expert users will find it adaptable. It's compatible with Windows, Mac, and Linux. Teachers' other professionals use it and students to create low-cost scientific equipment, demonstrate chemistry and physics concepts, and begin learning programming and robotics. Architects and designers create interactive prototypes, while musicians and artists utilize them to create installations and try new instruments. Makers, for example, utilize it to construct many of the items on display at the Maker Faire. Arduino is a valuable tool for learning new skills. Anyone - youngsters, amateurs, artists, programmers - may get started experimenting by studying the step-by-step instructions

For physical computing, there are a variety of additional microprocessors and microprocessor platforms to choose from. Similar functionality may be found in Parallax Basic Stamp, Phi-gets, Net-0media's BX-24, MIT's Handy-board, and many more programs. All of these programs condense the complicated elements of microcontroller programming into an easy-to-use package. Although Arduino simplifies designing with microcontrollers, it has several advantages over other instructors, students, and curious enthusiasts.

1.2 Types of Arduino Boards

Arduino is a fantastic platform for developing ideas and innovations, but choosing the proper board may be difficult. If you're new to Arduino, you may have assumed that there's just one "Arduino" board, and that was it. In truth, there are several versions of the genuine Arduino boards and hundreds of clones from rivals. But don't worry; later in this chapter, you will learn which one to start with. The following are some examples of the many kinds of Arduino boards available. The authentic Arduino boards are those with the Arduino logo on them, although there are many excellent clones on the marketplace. One of the main reasons to purchase a clone is that they are usually less costly than the original. For example, Spark Fun and Adafruit provide Arduino boards less expensive but have the same quality as the originals. One word of caution, be cautious when purchasing boards from unknown vendors.

Another thing to think about when picking a board is indeed the sort of project you want to accomplish. If you want to make a wearable electrical project, the Lilypad boards from Spark fun are a good option. The Lilypad is intended to be sewed into wearable and e-textiles crafts with ease. If your work has a compact form factor, the Arduino Pro Mini, which has a very tiny footprint comparing to other boards, can be a good choice. For analysis and analysis of the top boards available, see Spark fun's Arduino Comparison Guide. Following that, you'll look at our preferred Arduino board, which is suggested novices begin with.

Arduino Uno

The Arduino Uno is among the most famous Arduino boards. Even though it was not the first board to be launched, it is still the most popular and well-documented on the market. Because of its widespread usage, the Arduino Uno has many projects and forums available on the Internet to assist you in getting started or getting out of a bind. Because of its amazing features and simplicity of use, you love the Uno.

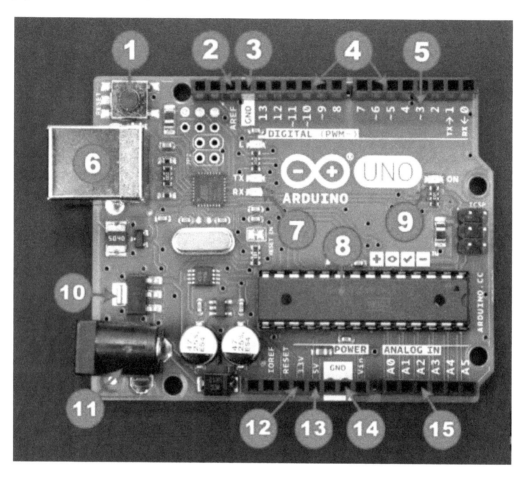

Breakdown of the Board

The components that comprise an Arduino UNO board are listed below, along with their functionalities.

- **Reset Button.** Pressing this button will reload any programming on the Arduino board.

- **AREF**. This acronym stands for "Analog Reference," which establishes an outside reference voltage.

- **Ground Pin**. The Arduino has many ground pins, all of which function in the same way.

- **PWM.** The pins indicated with the () symbol may emulate analog output.

- **USB Cable.** Used to power up the Arduino and upload programs.

- **TX/RX.** LEDs that indicate data transmission and reception.

- **AT Mega Microchip.** It is the brain of the board, which is where the programs are kept.

- **Power Indicator Light**. When the board is hooked into a power source, this LED illuminates.

- **Voltage Regulator.** It regulates the voltage supplied to an Arduino board.

- **3.3 volts Pin.** The Pin offers 3.3 hours of electricity to your work.

- **Dc Voltage Barrel Jack.** This Pin is used to power the Arduino with such a power source.

- **V Pin**. This Pin provides your projects with 5 volts of electricity.

- **Ground Pins.** The Arduino has several ground pins that all function the same way.

- **Analog Pins**. The pins can read analog sensor signals and transform them too digital.

Arduino Power Supply

The Arduino Uno requires a power supply to function and may be charged in several ways. You may connect the boards directly to your desktop using a USB connection, as most users do. Consider utilizing a 9V rechargeable battery to power your project if you want it to be portable. The last option is to utilize a 9V AC source of power.

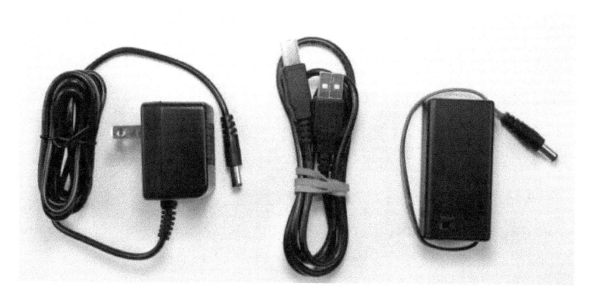

Arduino Breadboard

When working with Arduino, a solderless breadboard is also essential. You may use this gadget to develop your Arduino work without having to connect the circuit permanently. You may make additional prototypes and test with alternative circuit designs using a breadboard. Metal clips are joined via a strip of conductive material within the plastic housing slots (tie points).

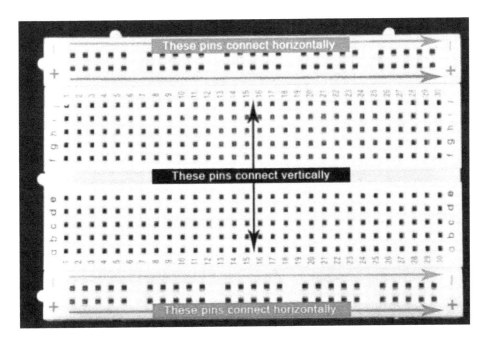

On a separate note, the breadboard does not have its power supply and must be connected to the Arduino board via jumper wires. These fibers are also used to link resistors, switches, and other elements to make the circuit.

1.3 Setting the Arduino Board

After you have studied the introduction of the Arduino and learned a bit about what You're programming, you'll learn how to install the software. You should turn on your computer and get started writing code. Getting Started When you purchase an Arduino board, it normally comes preloaded with an example Blink software that flashes the built-in light-emitting diode (LED). The LED is connected to one of the board's digital input-output ports. Digital pin 13 is linked to it. As a result, pin 13 can only be utilized as an output. However, since the LED only consumes a modest amount of electricity, you may still utilize that connection for other purposes. Using your Arduino start-up, all you have to do is connect it to a power source. The simplest method is to connect it to your computer's USB connection. You'll need a USB cable that converts from type A to type B. It's the same sort of cable that connects your computer to your printer. The LED should flash if everything is operating properly. This Blink sketch is pre-installed on new Arduino boards to ensure that the board is functional.

1.4 Installing the Software

You must do more than just give electricity to the Arduino board through USB to be required to activate fresh sketches. You should then upload a program to the Arduino board after successfully installing the Arduino board and, according to your system, USB drivers.

Putting Your First Sketch Online, the flashing LED is Arduino's version of the "Hello World" program, which is the usual first program to execute while learning a new language in other languages. Let's put the environment to the test by installing and changing this application on your Arduino board. When you first launch the Arduino computer, it displays an empty sketch.

Fortunately, the program comes with a large number of examples to get you started. So that's where the file menu comes in.

You must now upload or copy the sketch on your Arduino Uno board. So, using the USB cable, connect your Arduino board to your computer. The green LED on the Arduino should light up. An Arduino board will likely be blinking already since the Blink code is usually pre-installed on the boards. But first, let's reinstall it and then tweak it. If you're using a Macintosh, you could receive the notice "A network connection has been discovered" when you connect the board in. Simply click Cancel; the Mac is perplexed and believes the Arduino is a USB cable. You must inform the Arduino program what sort of board you use and whose serial port it connects to until you can load a sketch.

The serial port on a Windows computer is always COM3. On Linux or Macs PCs, the list of available serial devices is substantially larger). The device will usually appear at the top of the list, with a name that sounds like "/dev/tty.usbmodem621". Now, on the toolbar, click the Upload icon.   There is a little wait when you hit the button while the drawing is constructed before the transmission starts. If it's functioning, you should see a flurry of LED flashing while the sketch is transmitted, followed by the message "Done Uploading" at the foot of the Arduino program window and another message that says something like "Binary sketch size: 1018 bytes" (Maximum 14336 byte).

1.5 Arduino drivers

Arduino drivers must be installed. A USB port is available on Arduino boards. Before connecting the board to your computer through USB, you must first install appropriate drivers on the latter. There is a significant difference between OSX and Windows in this regard; OS X, for example, does not need any particular drivers for the Arduino Uno or the Mega 2560. If you're using an older board, you'll need to go to the FTDI website and download the current version of drivers, double-click the package, follow the instructions, and then restart your computer. You will study How it works with Windows computers, namely Windows 8,10 etc. Installing Arduino Uno R3 drivers to utilize the Arduino R3 and several other boards, you must first complete the procedures listed below. For the most up-to-date information, go to the Arduino website.

- Connect your board to the computer, then wait for Windows to complete the driver installation. The procedure eventually fails after a few seconds.

- Click the Start Button to open the control panel.

- Go to System & Security in the Control Panel. Then choose the system. Open Device Manager after the System window has shown.

- Look in the Ports section (COM & LPT). Examine the Arduino UNO open port (COMxx).

- Select Update Driver Software from the context menu of the Arduino UNO port.

- Next, choose to Browse your system for driver software from the drop-down menu.

- Finally, in the Arduino software download's Drivers folder, find and pick the Uno's driver file, titled ArduinoUNO.inf

- From there, Windows will complete the driver installation, and everything will be great.

1.6 C Language Basics

C is the programming language that is used to program Arduinos. You will learn the fundamentals of the C programming language. As an Arduino programmer, you'll use everything you've learned here to every sketch you create. These foundations are required to get the most out of Arduino.

People who speak other languages are not rare. In fact, and you study, the simpler it seems to be to acquire spoken languages, as you begin to see similar grammatical and lexical patterns. Programming languages are no exception. If you've ever used another programming language, you'll be able to take up C fast. The good news is that a programming language's vocabulary is far below that of a speaking language, but since you write it instead of speaking it, you can always check things up in the dictionary.

Furthermore, a programming language's grammar and syntax are remarkably consistent, and once you grasp a few basic principles, learning faster becomes second nature. An instruction—or a sketch, as the Arduino program is known—is best thought of as a series of instructions to be followed out in the order they are put down. Let's say you wanted to write something like this: Each of these three lines will do something. Pin 13's output would be set to HIGH in the first line. It is the Pin on the Arduino board with an LED built-in. Thus, the LED would light up at this point. The second line would patiently wait half a second before turning the LED off again, and the third line would do the same. As a result, these three lines will cause the LED to blink once. You've previously seen a surprising diversity of punctuation employed in unusual ways, as well as words with no spaces between them. "You know what You'd like to accomplish, but You don't know everything You need to write!" is a common dissatisfaction among inexperienced programmers. Don't worry, everything will be explained. First, let's take a look at the punctuation and how the words are created. Both of these elements are part of the language's syntax. Most languages demand exceptional precision in syntax, and one of the most important criteria is that object names must be one word. That is, they are unable to incorporate any spaces. So, digitalWrite is a brand name for a product. It's the name of a constructed function on the Arduino board that will set an output pin (you'll learn something about functions later). Names must not only be free of spaces, but they must also be case-sensitive. As a result, you must type digitalWrite rather than DigitalWrite or Digitalwrite. The function digitalWrite requires information about which port to set and whether that Pin should be set HIGH or LOW. These two data bits are referred to as arguments, and they are supplied to a function once it is called. A function's arguments must be separated by commas and surrounded in parentheses. The starting parenthesis should be placed directly after the final letter of the function's name, and space should be placed after the comma until the next argument. You may, however, use space characters inside the parenthesis if desired. There is no need for a comma if the function has only one parameter. Take note of the semicolon at the end of each line. Because the semicolon signals the conclusion of one instruction, similar to the conclusion of a sentence, it would have been more logical if they had been periods. You'll learn more about what occurs when you hit the Upload button also on the Arduino development environment in the following section (IDE).

1.7 Program writing for Arduino board

The Arduino Programming Language is a language that Arduino supports natively.

This program is based upon on Wiring development environment, which is based on Processing; it's what p5.js gets based on if you're unfamiliar with it. It has a rich history of projects growing on top of one other in an Open-Source manner. The Arduino IDE is primarily based on Processing IDE, which is based on the Wiring IDE.

When working with Arduino, you'll most likely use the Arduino Board Integrated Development Environment (IDE), a piece of software available for all major desktop environment (macOS, Windows, Linux) that provides us with two things: a programming editor with built-in libraries, and a way to quickly Load and compile our Arduino program onto a computer-connected board.

The Arduino Language is essentially a C++-based framework. You may argue that it isn't a true language of programming in the classic sense, but this helps newcomers avoid misunderstandings.

The sketch is the name for a program created in the Arduino Uno Programming Language. Normally, a drawing is stored with the ".ino" extension (from Arduino).

The key difference between it and "normal" C++ or C is that all of your code is wrapped into two primary functions. Of course, you may have more than two, but each Arduino program must have at least those two.

The first is known as setup (), and the second is known as a loop (). One is called first when your program begins, and the second is called "frequently" while running.

You don't have a main () function as you have in C/C++ as the program's entry point. When you compile your sketch, your IDE checks to see whether the final result is a valid C++ program and preprocesses it to add the missing glue.

Everything else is standard C++ code, and since C++ is a generalized form of C, any legitimate C code will work with Arduino.

One distinction that may create confusion is that, although you may launch your application over numerous files, they must also be in the folder. If your software becomes extremely big, this constraint may be a deal-breaker; however, at that time, it will be simple to switch to a local C++ arrangement, which is conceivable.

Built-in libraries are part of an Arduino Programming Language and enable you to quickly connect with the Arduino board's capabilities.

Your first Arduino program will almost certainly include turning on and off a light. You'll utilize the delay (), pinMode(), and digitalWrite() methods, as well as certain constants like LOW, HIGH, and OUTPUT, to do this.

1.8 Arduino sketch

You can probably identify an Arduino sketch and guess what it's attempting to accomplish, but you'll need to go a little further into how programming language code transforms from words on the page to something that can do anything, like turn an LED. "OFF" or "NO." This diagram depicts the whole process, from entering code into the Arduino IDE to executing the sketch on board.

When you hit the Upload button on the Arduino IDE, a series of actions occur, culminating in your sketch being installed and executed on the Arduino. It's not as simple as copying and pasting the text from the editor to an Arduino board. The first phase is a process known as compilation. It converts the code you've typed into machine code, which is the binary language that Arduino understands. When you use the Arduino IDE's triangle Verify button, it tries to compile the C code you've written instead of sending it all to the Arduino IDE. Compiling the code has the secondary benefit of ensuring that it plays by the rules of a C programming language.

Despite its Italian roots, the Arduino has attempted to assemble the words "Ciao Bella," but it has no clue what you're talking about. It is not a C text. Consequently, you get the puzzling warning "error: Ciao does not identify a type" at the edge of the screen. What this signifies is that there are several flaws in your writing.

Your attempts at creating code have been evaluated by the Arduino IDE and deemed to be acceptable. It informs you of this by announcing "Done Compiling" and providing you with the sketch's size: 450 bytes. The IDE also informs you that the maximum size equals 32,256 bytes, indicating that you have plenty of capacity to expand your drawing. Let's have a look at the source code that will serve as the foundation for every drawing you ever produce. There are a few new additions here. There's the term void, for example, as well as some curly brackets. Let's start with the emptiness.

You're creating a method named setup with the line void setup (). Some functions, such as delay and digitalWrite, are already specified for you in

Arduino, but you must or may create others. In every drawing you draw, you must specify two functions for yourself: setup and loop. The crucial thing to remember is that you are not using setup or loop in the same way that you would use digitalWrite; rather, you are constructing these functions so the Arduino system may call them. It is a tough notion to understand, but one thing to understand about it is as if you were reading a legal term.

Lawyers might make their papers shorter and more accessible by defining terms in the way—for example, using the word "author" as shorthand for "The person or individuals responsible for generating the book." Functions act in a similar way to definitions. You create a function that either you or your system may utilize in other parts of your drawings. Returning to void, as these two functions (loop and setup) may not return a value like some others, you must declare them void by using the void reserved words. If you imagine a function named sin that executed a trigonometric function of the same name, you'll see that it returns a value. The sin of an angle supplied as its parameter would be the value returned for using from the function. You construct functions using C that may then be called in C, similar to how a legal definition employs words to describe a term. The name of the function follows the special term void, followed by parentheses to hold any parameters. There are still no arguments in this situation, and the parenthesis must still be included. Because you are creating a function instead of calling it, there is no ";" semicolon after the ending parenthesis. You must state what will happen if the function is called.

Things that must happen when the function is invoked must be enclosed in curly brackets. A block of code is made up of curly brackets and the code that goes between them, and it's a notion you'll see again later. It's worth noting that you don't have to write any code in them though you must declare the functions loop and setup. Failure to include code, on the other hand, will make you're drawing a bit boring. Blink, Blink, Blink, Blink, Blink, Blink, B The setup and loop functions on Arduino are used to distinguish between tasks that must be completed just once, such as when the Arduino begins executing its sketch and tasks that must be completed repeatedly. When the sketch begins, the function setup will only be performed once. You should add additional code to it to make the LED on the board flash. After that, add the outlines to your sketch, look like this, and then publish it to your board.

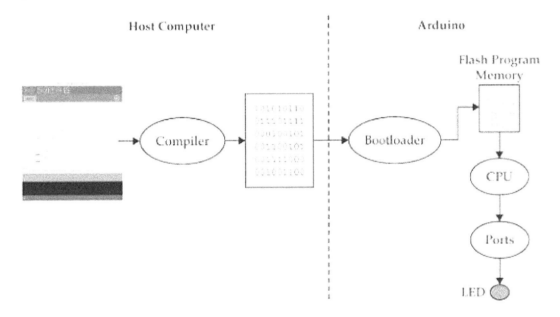

1.9 LCD Module with Arduino

Do you want to show status updates or sensor data on your Arduino projects? Then these LCD screens could be just what you're looking for. They're highly prevalent and a quick approach to give your product a legible interface.

You will learn everything you need to know about Character LCDs and how to use them. Not only 16 by 2(1602) but then any character Lcd screens (for example, 16 by 4, 16 by 1, 20 by 4, etc.) that use Hitachi's HD44780 parallel connection LCD controller chip. Because the Arduino team has already created a library for dealing with HD44780 LCDs, you'll be able to connect them in no time.

Liquid Crystal Display (LCD) is a display device that generates a visible picture using liquid crystals.

When current is sent through this unique kind of crystal, it becomes opaque, blocking the backlight from behind the screen. As a consequence, that specific region will seem darker than the others. That's how the characters appear on the screen.

1.10 Hardware Overview

The moniker "Character LCD" comes from the fact that LCDs are best for showing simply text or characters. The display features an LED backlight and can show 32 ASCII characters in 2 lines of 16, with each row displaying 16 characters.

You can see the small rectangles for every character on display, as well as the pixels that go up a character if you look carefully. Any one of these rectangles is a 588-pixel grid.

Although they show text, they are available in various sizes and colors, including 16 by 1, 16 by 4, 20 by 4, white color on a blue backdrop, black text on green, and many more.

The great news is that some of these screens are 'swappable,' meaning that if you create your project with one, you can simply unplug it and replace it with a different size/color LCD. Your code may need to change to accommodate the increased size, but the wiring remains the same! Let's have a look at the LCD Pinout before You go into the connections and sample code.

GND should be linked to Arduino's ground is the LCD's power source, which you connect to the Arduino's 5 volts pin. The LCD contrast and brightness are controlled by Vo (LCD Contrast). You may fine-tune the contrast by using a simple voltage divider and a potentiometer.

The RS (Register Select) pin tells the Arduino whether it's delivering instructions or data to the LCD. This Pin is mostly used to distinguish instructions from data.

When the RS pin is set at LOW, for example, you send orders to the LCD. When the RS pin is set to HIGH, data/characters are sent to the LCD.

The read/Write Pin upon on LCD is used to regulate whether you're reading and writing data to a display. You'll tie this pin LOW since you'll only be utilizing the LCD as just an OUTPUT device. It switches it to WRITE mode.

The display is turned on using the E (Enable) pin. When this Pin is set at LOW, the LCD is unconcerned with what is going on with the R/W, RS, and data bus lines; when it is set to HIGH, the LCD is analyzing the incoming data.

1.11 Testing Character LCD

You've arrived at the exciting part. Let's put your LCD to the test. Connect the Arduino Uno's 5V and GND pins to the board power rails, then plug your LCD into the breadboard. You'll now turn on the LCD. The LCD has two independent power connections: one for the LCD itself (Pin 1 and Pin 2), another for the LCD backlight (Pin 15 and Pin 16). Connect the LCD's pins 1 & 16 to GND and ports 2 and 15 to 5V.

Chapter 2: Arduino C

With the founding of the X3J11 commission in 1983, the C language started its journey to become legally standardized by the American National Standard Institute (ANSI). In 1989, the committee's work was done, and the standard was approved. Ever since the language has been dubbed "ANSI C." The ISO (International Organization for Standardization) has also accepted the standard. Hence, it is frequently referred to as "ISO C." ANSI C are the same. Both versions are also referred to as "standard C" in a culture obsessed with political correctness.

The C you're going to learn isn't your typical C. Instead, you'll learn a solid subset of conventional C. There are a few C features that aren't present. However, the lack of such qualities is by no means a fatal blow. You'll quickly realize that the Arduino C subset of normal C is more than capable of handling just about any job you could throw at it. The lack of features may readily be compensated for, though in a less attractive way.

2.1 Building Blocks

From Ada to ZPL, all programming languages are made up of four essential elements:

- Expression:
- Statements
- Blocks of statements
- Function Blocks

The fourth portion, function blocks, is known by a variety of names in a different language, including "methods" in Java, C++ "procedures" in Pascal, "subroutines" in Basic or Fortran, and potentially a more obscure title in lesser-known languages. Function blocks, regardless of their name, are code blocks that perform a certain task. Programs are just a collection of these elements that have been structured in a way that solves issues.

Expression:

Pairing operands and operators yield an expression. An operand, simply put, is a set of data that is operated on with an operator. A logical or mathematical action performed on one or more operands is known as an operator.

Examples of expressions are x + y, a −12 r> you. In the first case, the operands x and y are joined together in a math operation using the + operator. The numerical constant 12 (an operand) is subtracted (a − operator) from the operand labeled an in the second example. Operand r is compared to operand d in the previous example to see whether u is smaller than (the operator) d. Rather than a math operator, the relational operator (e.g., the "less than" operator, or) is used in the final example. The two operands are combined with the single operator to generate an expression in all three instances. An addition expression is the first, a subtraction expression is the second, and a relationship expression is the third.

There are two operands and one operator in these expressions. As a result, such expressions are often referred to as binary operator expressions. Binary operators (for example, +, −, and) always have two operands. Another thing to remember is that every expression will resolve to a value at some point. (Some unary operators only need one operand, and ternary operators need three.) The binary operators, on the other hand, are the most popular in C.

Expressions may be mixed and matched. Consider the following scenario: x = 1, y = 2, and z = 3. A complicated expression may be written as x+y +z.

Because all equations have a value, you may solve the first one, x +y, which can be simplified to 11 + 12 + z.

Because the first phrase is now entirely of integers, it may be resolved to the value 3.

The complicated phrase may then be reduced to 3 + z

Take note of what occurred here. You resolved one of the expressions (i.e., x + y) into three from a complicated expression containing two operators and three operands. However, you simplified the complicated expression to a simple expression, 3 + C, in the process. The remaining equation may now be written as

3 + C.

3+3 =6

The complicated expression with two subexpressions is now resolved to a single value, 6, and the complicated expression with two sub-expressions is now resolved to a single value, 6. This process of reducing a complicated expression is sometimes referred to as factoring or resolving an expression.

How about g< d, a relational expression? If r= 15 and u = 14, the equation is: r<u false

Because 15 is larger than 14, not less than 14, the expression evaluates too false.

"Wait a minute!" you could exclaim. All expressions you just mentioned evaluates to a value. "False" is a word, not a value." True. However, logic false and logic true expressions in programming languages do resolve to a value. Logic true evaluates to a non-zero number (e.g., –1) in most languages, whereas logic false resolves to zero.

Because relational expressions are built to evaluates to a logic False or true state, they will eventually resolve to a value that can be utilized in a program.

Statement

A statement is indeed a full computer C instruction. A semicolon is used after every C statement (;). Here is some example of C statements:

s= 50;

x = y + z;

a = b / 2;

The assignment operator (=) is used to "assign" the value on the right side of the equation to the operand upon the equal sign's left side in the first example.

As a result, variable s is given the value 50 in the first sentence. Note that the first statement is nothing more than an assignment operator expression with a semicolon at the end of the line. 50 and variable s are the operands. A variable is nothing other than a memory region that has been given a name.

You have a complicated phrase with such a semicolon at the end of the second sentence. Because the result to assign to variable an is unknown in this example, you must first resolve the phrase x + y to get a value. If x = 14 and z=15, the complicated statement may be reduced to x = y + z x = 14+15 x = 29

Variable an is assigned the value 29 in the final phrase. By adding a semicolon at the end of the statement, the expression is transformed into a statement that changes the value of variable a to 29. On the other hand, the semicolon causes the C compiler to complete whatever work the statement requires. If you have a complicated statement like x = y+ z −c+h+j+m, the compiler must first resolve all intermediate expressions (a+b,c+g,h k) before determining what new value to assign x.

Statement Blocks

A statement block is made up of one or even more statements that have been grouped such that the compiler treats them as if they were a single statement. Assume you're apartment management, and there's 3 inches or more of snow; you'll need to shovel the walkway. You might write it like this (the >= operator means "greater than or equal to "):

```
if (snow>=3) {
Put_On_Snow_Removal_Stuff();
Get_Snow_Shovel();
Shovel_Side_walk();
} else {
Go_Back_To_Bed();
}
```

An initial brace character "{" precedes a statement block, which is followed by a closing brace character. A statement block body is made up of all statements between both the open or closed braces. In our example, You seem to put on your coats, get a shovel, and snow shovel the sidewalks when there are three or more inches of snow. A separate statement block is run. There is smaller than 3 inches of snow (i.e., You go back to bed). Within the statement block, you may put whatever form of statement you want. In the following chapters, you'll see a number more instances of this. Consider a statement block to be defined by opening and closing braces for the time being.

Function Blocks

The function block would be a snippet of code that performs a single function. You utilized the function block throughout the preceding section, even though you weren't aware of it. Put_On_Snow_Removal_Stuff(), in other words, is a method that instructs you to put on your coat. The real code may look something like this:

```
void_Put_On_Snow_Removal_Stuff(void) {
if (Not_Dressed) {
 Put_On_Clothes();
 Put_On_Shoes();
}
Go_To_Closet();
Put_On_Boots();
Put_On_Coat();
Put_On_Gloves();
Put_On_Hat();
}
```

The function block in this example similarly begins with an initial brace and finishes with a closing brace. On the other hand, function blocks are often created to create "black boxes," The specifics of how You accomplish anything are hidden inside the function. You may be considering building the code for a robot that will need sensors to detect what is ahead. You may create a TurnRight() method that causes your robot to turn 90° to the right. It most likely entails rotating one of the wheels, maybe by increasing the voltage applied to a stepper motor, causing the front wheels to move to the right. However, you may elect to modify your robot's wheels from four to three at a later time. You no longer need to spin two wheels; just one is required. Because the intricacies of turning your robots to the right are hidden in the Turn Right () black box, you have only to alter the program code in one place rather than a variety of locations where a right turn could be required. You may avoid repeating all of the TurnRight() method instructions on each occasion a right turn is required in the application by developing a TurnRight() function.

Another illustration could be useful. Assume you're creating an application that takes a phone number from a keypad and enters it into a database. Home, mobile, and work phone numbers are required for your application. To ensure that a legitimate phone number was input, make sure it follows the "1-000-000-0000" format. You could neither construct a Check_Phone_Format() method and call it three times, or you could replicate the format checking program code three times throughout the application. Let's have a look... Create the code three times, test it, debug it, or write a function once and debug it. To me, it seems to be a no-brainer. Additionally, by avoiding repeating the code, you will use fewer memory resources while calling functions.

If you consider a computer program as a series of smaller activities, you'll see that function blocks are utilized to separate the code for each one of them. The Arduino programming language offers hundreds, if not hundreds, of pre-written function blocks, which you may utilize in your applications, as you will soon discover. It implies you won't have to innovate every time you encounter a typical programming job.

You copy and paste an existing function block from the library of pre-written function blocks into your software. Since you can walk on the shoulders of developers who have already committed to a C++ library that you can use, life is nice and frequently simpler!

Every program you can imagine is made up of the four fundamental components covered in the section. Indeed, the remainder of the book is devoted to demonstrating how to utilize these basic components to solve a specific programming issue. However, therein is the issue. There are endless ways to put these pieces together in a computer program, some of which will function and others that will not. Just because your software works doesn't imply, there isn't a better (or more efficient?) method to do the same goal. Consider the following scenario: you would like to sort a collection of numbers into a list from the least to the greatest number inside the group. There are several methods for sorting a list of integers into ascending order, each with its own set of benefits and drawbacks. In fact, as your study something about programming in general, you'll discover that your options expand. Even basic tasks like scanning a series of text for a certain pattern may be accomplished in various methods. More the programming knowledge and expertise you gather, the more elegant solutions to programming problems you will be able to create. After all, if your primary instrument is a hammer, it's not a surprise that all of your issues resemble nails.

Furthermore, as the difficulty of a job grows, so does the number of possible solutions. If someone asked you to create fire alarms for a hotel, you'd probably come up with a million different ideas.

2.2 The Five-step C Arduino programing

Every program you can conceive of can be broken down into five fundamental phases or parts. When you're initially starting to build a program, think about it in terms of the Five Program Steps listed below.

Initialization Step

The Initialization Step's objective is to set up the environment where the application will execute. If you've used word or other comparable applications, you'll notice that the File command typically displays a list of the most frequently used files. You may set a home page in most web browsers. A default printer is typically included with a print application. A database software often establishes a preset network connection. Data is collected from someplace (e.g., a data file, RAM, EEPROM, or the registry) in each of these circumstances and utilized to create a basic environment where the program will execute.

Simply said, the Initialization Step performs any necessary background preparations before the program may begin executing to do its core job.

Input Step

Almost every computer program contains a job that takes a present condition of information, processes it somehow, and displays the new state of such information. If you're creating a fire suppression system, you'll take the data supplied by the flame sensors, assess their present status, and take action if there's a fire. If the sensor does not detect a fire, the procedure may be repeated with a second range of nodes. Indeed, your software may do nothing for decades except take fresh data every few seconds and evaluate if any corrective action is required. Regrettably, the day may arrive when a fire occurs, and immediate action is required. Nonetheless, the whole process is dependent on the timely entry of new data from the sensors.

The Input Phase is the set of program statements required to get the data required to complete the job at hand.

Process Step

Continuing using our fire alarm software, after the sensors' input is received, some code should be responsible for identifying whether or not the sensors have detected a fire. In other words, to ascertain the present condition of the sensors, the voltage (i.e., temperature) should be input and afterward interpreted (e.g., the data processed). Perhaps the data entered inside a desktop application is the price & quantity of an item bought by a consumer. The Process Step can be in charge of calculating the final cost to the customer. It's worth noting that software may contain many Process Steps. For example, determining the sales tax payable on a transaction may be a procedure with our customer. The procedure of calculating the total cost of the transaction becomes an output to calculate the sales tax owed in this situation. Another method might use the sales and tax owed as inputs.

On the other hand, the Process Step is in charge of accepting several objects and processing them to produce a new collection of data in all circumstances.

Output Step

The final value is generally output on a display device when the Processing Element has completed its task. In our consumer sales scenario, You might now show the entire amount owed to us by the customer. The Output Step, on the other hand, isn't only about showing the new data. New data is often stored or passed along to another application. For instance, the software may collect sales data during the day and update data at night so that another software can prepare purchase orders for management to see the following morning. Under typical settings, the Output Step in the fire alarm instance may cause an LED for a specific sensor to show a green hue. If a fire occurs, the LED may turn red, allowing those in charge to see which part of the structure is on fire.

The Output Phase is in charge of putting the Process Step's results to good use. This application might be as simple as showing the current information on a monitor screen or transferring the new value to another software.

Termination Step

After the program has completed its mission, the Termination Step is responsible for "cleaning up." In a desktop program, the Termination Step often performs the Initialization Step "backward." In that instance, if the program maintains a list of the most recently utilized data files, the Termination Step should update that list. If the Initializing Step establishes a database and printer connection, the Termination Step must terminate that connection to free up system resources.

Many mc programs, on the other hand, are not intended to be terminated. As long as conditions are "normal," a fire alarm is likely to keep working indefinitely. Even then, there may be a Termination Process in place. For example, if a component throughout the fire alarm fails, the Session may attempt to locate the faulty component until the system is shut down for repairs. Before a maintenance shutdown, the Termination Process may disable the alarm system.

2.3 Arduino C Data Types

With a few significant exceptions, Arduino C supports the majority of ANSI C data types. There's also some hanky-panky with floating - point, but that shouldn't be an issue if you understand what's going on "under the hood."

A variable is nothing more than a slice of storage that was given a name. When you declare a variable, you must also specify the kind of data associated with it. The type of data of even a variable is significant because it dictates however many bytes of memory are allocated to it, and what types of data may be stored in it. There are two fundamental categories of data: values types and reference types, as you'll see later in this chapter. If the variable is declared as just a value type, a very narrow range of values is also conceivable.

2.4 Keywords in C

Any term that has particular significance to a C compiler is referred to as a keyword. You can't utilize keywords with your function or variable names since they're reserved for the compiler. When you do, a compiler may report you as having made a mistake. If the compiler did not flag such mistakes, it would be unsure which keywords to employ in any given case.

Chapter 3: Functions

This chapter focuses on the functions you can create instead of the built-in functions like delay and digitalWrite that are already specified for you. You should develop your functions because as your drawings get more involved, your loop and setup routines will get longer and more sophisticated, making it harder to understand how they operate. The most difficult aspect of any software development project is dealing with complexity. The finest programmers create software that is simple to look at and comprehend, with little explanation required. Functions are an important tool for producing simple, easy-to-understand drawings that may be altered without difficulty or the danger of the whole document collapsing. What is the definition of a function? A function is similar to a program inside a program in that it is a program inside a program. It may be used to do any little task you have. A defined function may be called anywhere in the sketch and has its own set of variables and directives. After the instructions have been executed, execution resumes where it left off in the program that invoked the function. For instance, code that flashes the LED (light-emitting diode) is an excellent example of code that belongs in a function. So, let's update our simple "blink 20 times" sketch to include a method you'll name flash:

So, all you've done is relocate the four pieces of text that flash the LED from the "for-loop" midsection to a flash function. You now can create the LED flash whenever you want by just putting flash to the new function (). After the function name, notice the empty parenthesis. It means that the function has no input arguments. The delay value is determined by the delay period function, which you used before. Variables When breaking your drawing into functions, it's helpful to consider what kind of service each function may give. It is quite clear in the instance of flash. But this time, let's give this function some arguments that tell it how many repetitions to flash and how brief or long to flash. After you've gone through the code below, you will go through how parameters operate in more depth.

```
int ledPin = 13;
int delayPeriod = 250;

void setup()
{
  pinMode(ledPin, OUTPUT);
}

void loop()
{
  flash(20, delayPeriod);
  delay(3000);
}

void flash(int numFlashes, int d)
{
  for (int i = 0; i < numFlashes; i ++)
  {
    digitalWrite(ledPin, HIGH);
    delay(d);
    digitalWrite(ledPin, LOW);
    delay(d);
```

If you check the loop function now, you'll see that it just contains two lines. You've delegated the majority of the job to a flash function. Notice how you now provide two parameters in parentheses to flash when you call it. You must identify the type of variable in the arguments when you specify the function at the sketch base. They're both integers in this scenario. In reality, you're creating new variables.

On the other hand, the variables number Flashes may only be utilized inside the flash function. It is a useful function since it contains all of the information required to flash a LED. The only information it requires from outside the function is the Pinto to which the LED is connected. You could also make it a parameter if you wanted to, which would be useful if you could have more than one LED connected to your Arduino.

Functions enable you to break down the program into smaller chunks of code that accomplish specific functions. When you need to do the same action numerous times in a program, you should create a function.

Organizing code fragments in functions provides several benefits.

- Functions aid in the programmer's organization. It often helps in the conceptualization of the program.
- Functions codify one operation in one place, reducing the number of times a function must be thought about it and debugged, as well as the number of times the code must be modified.
- Because chunks of code are reused several times, functions make the entire sketch shorter and more compact.
- They make it simpler to reuse code in other programs by making it modular, and they make it more understandable by employing functions.

In an Arduino sketch or program, setup () and loop () are essential functions; further functions must be written outside the parentheses of these two procedures.

3.1 Function Declaration

A function is defined above or below the loop function, outside of any other functions.

There are two methods to define the function.

The first method is to simply write the component of the function known as a function prototypes just above loop function, which comprises the following:

- The return type of a function

- Function name

- Function argument type (the argument name does not need to be written)

A semicolon must follow the function prototype (;).

```
int sum_function(int a, int y) // "function declaration"

{

int c = 0;

c =a+b;

return c; // return the integer value

}

void setup ()

{Statements // set of statements

}


Void loop(){

int result = 0;

result = Sum_function (15,61); // "calling of a function"

}
```

The second portion, known as the function Declaration or definition, should be declared just after the loop function, which is made from:

- Function return type

- Function name

- Function argument type, where the argument name must be included

- The body's function (when function is calling the statements inside the function will execute)

The following example shows how to use the second technique to declare a function.

```
int sum_function (int,int ) ; // function_prototype
void setup(){
   Statements // sets of statements
}
void loop(){
   int result= 0;
   result = Sum_function(15,61); // function calling
}


int sum_func (int x, int y) // function declaration {
   int z = 0;
   z = x+y ;
   return z; // return the value
}
```

The second method just declares the function above the loop function.

3.2 Built-in Functions

In this part, you will give a reference for the Arduino Programming Language's built-in functions.

Program lifecycle

- Setup () is called once when the program begins and again when the Arduino gets turned off and on.
- While the Arduino program is running, the loop () function is called repeatedly.

3.3 Handling I/O

The following routines assist you in managing your Arduino device's input and output.

Digital Input/Output

- **Digital Read():** It reads a digital pin's value. Returns the Low or High constant when given a PIN as an input.

- **DigitalWrite():** It sets the value of a digital output signal pin to Low or high the PIN and HIGH or LOW, given as parameters.

- **PinMode():** It determines whether a pin is an input or an output. As arguments, you supply the PIN and the OUTPUT or INPUT value.

- **Pulse In():** It reads a digital pulse on a pin from High to Low and back to High, or from low to high and back to low. Until the pulse is detected, the program will halt. You choose the pin code and the kind of pulse to detect (HLH or LHL). To cease waiting for that pulse, you may provide an optional timeout.

- **PulseInLong():** It is the same as pulse in (), except that it is implemented uniquely and cannot be used whenever disabled. Interrupts are often disabled to get a more precise result.

- **Shifting():** It reads a piece of data from a pin one bit at a time.

- **Shift Out():** It writes one bit by bit to a pin a byte of data.

- **Tone():** It delivers a square wave on a pin used to play tones on buzzers and speakers. You may choose the Pin as well as the frequency. It is compatible with both digital and analog pins.

- On a pin, No Tone () disables the tone () produced wave.

Analog Input/Output

- **Analog Read ():** It reads an analog pin's value.
- **Analog Reference ():** It sets the value for the analog input's top input range by defaulting 5 volts on 5-volt boards and 3.3 volts on 3.3 volts boards.
- **Analog Write():** It is a function that writes an analog value to a pin.
- **AnalogReadResolution():** It modifies the default analog bit resolution for analog Read (),set to 10 bits by default. Only on certain devices does it operate (Arduino Zero, MKR and Due)
- **AnalogWriteResolution():** It modifies the default analog bits resolution for analog Write (),set to 10 bits by default. Only on certain devices does it operate (Arduino Zero, MKR and Due)

3.4 Time functions

- **delay():** It stops the program for the supplied number of milliseconds. Postponement Microseconds () stops the application for a given number of microseconds.
- **Micros ():** It indicates the number of microseconds because the program began. Due to overload, it resets after 70 minutes.
- **Millis ():** It indicates the number of milliseconds because the program began. Due to overload, it resets after 50 days.

3.5 Math functions

- **abs()**: It returns a number's absolute value; restrict() limits a number's range; see use
- **map():** It remaps several one ranges to another; for more information, see use.
- **Max ()**: It returns the sum of two numbers.
- **Min ():** It returns the smaller of two values.
- **Pow ()**: It returns the net present value multiplied by a power.
- **sq()** It returns the square of an integer; sqrt() returns the square root of an integer.
- **Cos ():** It returns the cosine of an angle given.
- **Sin ():** It returns the sine of an angle given.
- **Tan ()** It returns the tangent of an angle given.

3.6 characters functions

- **alphanumeric():** It determines if a char is an alpha (a letter) or alphanumeric (a number or letter)
- **Ascii()**: It determines if a char is an ASCII character
- **isControl()**: It determines if a char is a control character
- **isDigit():** It determines if a char is a number
- **isGraph()**: It determines whether a char is a printed ASCII character with content (not space, for example).
- **isHexadecimal():** It determines whether a char is a hexadecimal value.
- **isLowerCase():** It tests whether a character in lowercase letters (A to F 0 to 9) • Digit() tests whether a char is a hexadecimal digit (A to F 0 to 9).
- **isPrintable()**: It determines if a char is a printed ASCII character.
- **isPunct():** It determines if a character is a punctuation character (a semicolon, a comma, an exclamation mark etc.)

- **isSpace():** It determines if a character is a space, a form feed, a newline, a carriage return, a horizontal tab, or a vertical tab.
- **isUpperCase():** It determines if a character is an upper-case letter
- **isWhitespace():** It determines if a character is a space letter or a horizontal tab

3.7 Random numbers

- random(): It returns a pseudo-random number

- randomSeed(): It sets an arbitrary beginning value for the pseudo-random number generator.

It's hard to generate random numbers in Arduino, as it is in other languages, and the series is the same, so either seed it with the present time or (in the instance of Arduino) receive the input from such an analog port.

3.8 bits and bytes

- **bit():** It returns the bit value ("0 = 1", "1 = 2", "2 = 4", "3 = 8"...)
- **bitClear():** It clears a numeric variable (sets it to 0). Accepts a number as well as the bit number, beginning from the right.
- **bitRead():** It reads a single digit from an integer. Accepts a number as well as the bit number, beginning from the right.
- **bitSet():** It sets a bit of an integer to one. Accepts a number as well as the bit number, beginning from the right.
- **bitWrite():** It assigns a value one or Zero to a single bit of an integer. Accepts a number, a bit number beginning on the right, as well as the value to write (Zero or 1)
- **highByte(:)** It returns the word variable's high-order (leftmost) byte (which has 2 bytes)

- **lowByte():** It has the low-order (rightmost) byte of a word variable using (which has 2 bytes)

3.9: Interrupts

- **noInterrupts():** Interruptions are disabled when is used.

- **attachInterrupt():** It allows an input signals pin to be used as an interrupt after being deactivated by interrupts(). Check the official documents to see what pins are authorized on each board. It enables an interrupt; detachInterrupt() disables it ()

Chapter 4: Arrays and Strings

An array is a group of variables that may be retrieved by using an index number. Arrays may be sophisticated in the C++ that Arduino sketches are created in, but utilizing basic arrays is easy, and Strings are being used to store text. They may be used to show text through an LCD or in the Serial Monitor window of the Arduino IDE. Arrays of characters are the same as the characters used in C programming, are also handy for storing user input. The Arduino String is a program that allows us to utilize a string object.

4.1 Arrays

Arrays are a kind of data structure. Arrays are a kind of data structure that can hold a range of items. So far, all of the variables you've seen have only had one value, generally an int. On the other hand, an array has a range of items, and you may access any of them by their position in terms. C, like the majority of computer languages, starts indexing positions at 0 instead of 1. As a result, the first item is the zeroth element. To demonstrate the usage of arrays, construct an example program that allows the Arduino board's built-in LED to flash "SOS" in Morse code repeatedly. In the nineteenth and twentieth centuries, the Morse code was an important mode of communication. Morse code may be conveyed through telegraph lines, through a radio connection, or utilizing signaling lights since it encodes letters as a succession of short and long dots. The letters "SOS" (an abbreviation for "save our souls") are still used as a distress signal across the world. Three small lights (dots) depict the letter "S," whereas three extended flashes depict the letter "O." (dashes). To keep track of the length of each flash, you'll utilize an array of int. After that, you could use the for loop to walk over each item in the array, flashing for the proper amount of time. Let's start by looking at how you'll construct an array of int holding the durations. By adding [] after a variable's name, you may indicate that it includes an array. In this situation, the values and durations will be set when the array is created. Curly braces are used as a starting point, followed by values separated by commas. Remember to use a semicolon at the back of the line. The square bracket syntax may be used to access any member in the array. For example, if you wish to obtain the first element of an array, you may write: Let's establish an array and print out all of its contents to the Serial port to demonstrate this.

With arrays, you must be cautious since the compiler would not attempt to prevent you from accessing data beyond the array's end. The arrays are a reference to a memory location. Data, including conventional variables and arrays, are kept in memory by the program. Computer memory is far more strictly organized than human memory. It's easy to conceive of an Arduino's memory as a series of pigeonholes. When you create an array of nine items, for example, the next nine pigeon holes are set aside for it, as well as the variable is said to refer to the array's initial pigeonhole or element. Returning to our earlier point about accessing data outside of your array's limits, you would still get an int from memory if you wanted to read durations [10]. However, the value of this int might be anything.

4.2 Example Of an arrays

```
int array_name[ 10 ] ; //an array with ten variables

void setup()

{

}

void loop () {

    for (int a = 1; a <= 10; a++ )
```

```
{
    Array_name[a] = 1;
    Serial.print (a);
    Serial.print ('\r');
  }
  for ( int x = 1; x <= 10; ++x )
{
    Serial.print (array_name[x]);
    Serial.print ('\r');
  }
}
```

An equal-to(=) sign and a brace-delimited semicolon list of initializers may also be used to initialize the array elements in the array definition. An initializer list is used to create an integer array containing ten values (line a), then printed in a tabular fashion.

```
int array_name [10] ={ 132, 127, 164, 118, 195, 114, 190, 170, 160, 137 };
void setup(){
}
void loop(){
for ( int x =1; x < =10; ++x ) {
Serial.print (x);
Serial.print('\r') ;
```

```
}
for ( int a =1; a<=10; ++a ){
Serial.print (array_name[a]) ;
Serial.print ('\r') ;
}
}
```

Arrays are crucial to Arduino and therefore should be given greater consideration. An Arduino programmer should understand the following key array ideas.

Arrays Passed to Functions

To send an array parameter to a function, just type the array's name without the brackets.

Arrays (Multi-Dimensional)

Arrays having two dimensions (i.e., subscripts) are often used to depict tables of values with rows and columns of data.

4.3 String

Text is stored using strings. They may be used to show text over an LCD or in the Serial Monitor window of the Arduino IDE. Strings may also be used to store user input. For instance, the characters which a user writes on an Arduino-connected keypad.

In Arduino programming, there are two sorts of strings:

- Arrays of characters that are the same as strings in C programming.
- The Arduino String object, which allows us to utilize a text string in our sketches.

4.4 Character Arrays

The first sort of string you'll study is a string that consists of a sequence of char characters. You learned what an array, a sequence of the same kind of data stored in memory. A string is a collection of character variables.

A string is a specialized array with an important addition at the end of a string that is always set to 0. (zero). A zero at the end is known as "null terminated string"

Example

```
void setup(){
Char my_string [7];
Serial.Begin(9600);
my_string[0] = 'A';
my_string[1] = 'b';
my_string [2] = 'c';
my_string [3] = 'd';
my_string [4] = 'e';
my_string [5] = 0; // "null terminator"
Serial.println(my_string);
}
void loop(){
}
```

The following example demonstrates a string composed of a character array containing printable characters with 0 as the array's final member to indicate that the string terminates here. Utilizing Serial. println() and giving the string's name, the string may be printed to an IDE of Arduino Serial Monitor window.

```
void setup(){
char my_string [] = "Coding";
Serial.begin(9600);
Serial.println(my_string);
}
void loop ()
{
}
```

4.5 Manipulating String Arrays

As seen in the following sketch, you may change a string array inside a drawing.

```
void setup(){
char love [] = " You love Coding";
Serial.begin(9600); // (1) printing the string
Serial.println(love); // (2) deleting the string
love[2] = 0;
Serial.println(love);    //(3) substitute string
love [13] = ' ';
love[18] = 'b'; // insert the new word
love[19] = "o";
```

```
love[20] = 'o';

love[21] = k;

Serial.println(love);

}

void loop() {

}
```

Result

You love coding

You Love

4.6 reducing the length of the string

By changing the 14th letter inside the string("I like cake and coffee") with a "null" means ending zero, the length is shortened (2). It is the thirteenth entry in the string array, counting from zero. All characters in the string are written up to a new null ending zero when it is printed. The remaining characters do not vanish; they remain in memory, or the string array remains the same size. The only distinction is that any string-related function will only view the string until it reaches a first null terminator.

4.7 Exchange of "Words."

Finally, the term "cake" is replaced with "tea" in the drawing (3). It must first substitute the "null terminator" at example[12] with such a space to return the string to its original format. New characters replace the letter "cak" in the term "cake" with the letter "tea." Individual characters are overwritten to do this. A new null ending character replaces the "e" in "cake." Consequently, the string is ended with two "null characters," one at the end of a string and the other replacing the "e" in "cake." When the new string is written, this makes no impact since the string characters' function terminates when it meets the first "null terminator."

```
void setup(){
char example[] = "I like cake and coffee";
Serial.begin(9600);
Serial.println(example);
example[12] = 0;
Serial.println(example);


  like[12] = ' ';
  like[13] = 'd'; // new word
  like[14] = 'i';
  like[15] = 'n';
  like[16] = 0; // terminate the string
  Serial.println(example);
}
void loop() {
}
```

Result

I like cake and coffee

I like cake

I like coffee and din

4.8 Length of an Array

The size of the array, which includes the string, is obtained using the operation size of (). The length contains the null terminator; therefore, it is one longer than the string's length. Size of () seems to be a function, but it is an operator. It is not part of the C strings library, but it was used during the sketch to demonstrate the difference between array and string sizes (or string length).

4.9 Copy of an array

To copy my string [] string to your string[] array, use the strcpy () function. The strcpy () method replaces the initial string with the second string provided to it. You still have 23 free char parts in the array since a duplicate of the string exists in your string[] array, but it only takes up 19 of the array's 18 members. These free items are found in memory following the string.

The string was transferred to the array so that there would be enough room in the array for the following portion of the sketch, which is attaching a string to the end of the string.

To a String, append a String (Concatenate). Concatenation is the process of joining two strings together in the drawing. "The strcat ()" function is used to do this. The strcat () method appends the second string it receives to end the first text it receives. The length is displayed after concatenation to illustrate the format string length. The array's length is then reported, indicating that you have a 26-character string in a 40-element array; because of the null ending zero, a 25-character long string occupies 26 characters of an array.

```
void setup(){
char my_string[] = "First string is mine";
char your_string [40];
```

```
int nu;

Serial.begin(9600);

Serial.println(str);

nu = strlen(str);

Serial.print("String length is: ");

Serial.println(num);

nu= sizeof(str);

Serial.print("Size of the array: ");

 Serial.println(nu);

strcpy(your_string, str);

Serial.println(your_string);

strcat(your_string, " sketch.");

Serial.println(your_string);

nu= strlen(your_string);

Serial.print("String length is: ");

Serial.println(nu);

  nu= sizeof(your_string);

  Serial.print("Size of your_string []: ");

  Serial.println(nu);
}

void loop(){

}
```

4.10 Array Bounds

When dealing with strings & arrays, staying inside the constraints of the strings or arrays is critical. In the sample sketch, a 40-character array was built to allocate memory that can be used to edit strings.

If you attempted to copy the string larger than the array because the array was too tiny, the string would've been copied so over the end of the array. Other critical data utilized in the sketch may be stored in the memory further than the end of the array, which the string would overwrite. Unless the memory far beyond the end of a string is exceeded, the sketch may crash or behave unexpectedly.

Chapter 5 The Standard Arduino Library

There are several additional libraries and operating systems for various types of devices available. These drivers may be found on sites such as Github, Arduino Playground and CGoogle Code.

User-installed libraries should be placed into your sketchbook library folder so that they may be used with any IDE version. You won't have had to reinstall all of your favorite libraries whenever the latest version of an IDE is released!

5.1 Data storage

An Arduino sketch is saved in flash memory (program space). When the sketch runs, it generates and manipulates variables in SRAM; EEPROM is a kind of memory that programmers may utilize to save long-term data.

The microcontroller used in Arduino boards has three memory pools:

- An Arduino sketch is saved in flash memory (program space).
- When the sketch runs, it generates and manipulates variables in SRAM
- An EEPROM is a kind of memory that programmers may utilize to store long-term data.

A non-volatile memory such as flash memory and EEPROM, SRAM is a volatile memory that will be erased if the power is turned off. The ATmega328P chip in the Arduino has the following memory capacities. In a flash 32 kilobits, SRAM is a company that makes semiconductors. 2,000 bytes 1k byte EEPROM

Examples

- Bridge: Use a web browser to access the board's pins.
- ASCII Table for the Console: This shows how to print different formats to a Console.
- Console Pixel: Use the Console to control an LED.

- Console Read: Parse and repeat information from the Console.
- Datalogger: Save sensor data to an SD card.
- File Create Script: This shows how to use the process to write and run a shell script.
- HTTP Client: Make a basic client that downloads and outputs a site to the serial monitor.
- HTTP Client Console: Using Console, create a basic client which downloads a site and outputs it to a serial monitor.
- Mailbox Read Messages: Use a browser to send messages to an Arduino microcontroller using the REST API.
- Process: Shows how to perform Linux commands using process.

5.2 EEPROM Library

Enables reading and writing to the permanent board storage

- EEPROM Clear: The bytes inside the EEPROM are cleared.

- EEPROM Read: It Reads the details of the EEPROM and transfers them to the PC.

- EEPROM Write: Writes values to the EEPROM from an analog input.

- EEPROM Crc: Computes the CRC of the contents of an EEPROM chip as if it were an array.

- EEPROM Get: Gets values from an EEPROM and displays them on serial as floats.

- EEPROM Iteration: Learn how to iterate over the memory regions of an EEPROM.

- EEPROM Put: Using variable semantics, write values to EEPROM.

- EEPROM Update: Increases EEPROM life by storing values read from A0 in EEPROM and only writing the value if it differs.

5.3 Esplora Library

Allows simple access to the Esplora's many sensors and actuators.

- Esplora Accelerometer: It Read the accelerometer's readings.
- Esplora Blink: A Esplora's RGB LED will blink.
- Esplora Joystick Mouse: Control the mouse on your computer using Esplora's Joystick.
- Esplora LED Show: Make a light show with LED using the Joystick and slider.
- Esplora Led Show 2: Change the color of the onboard LED using the mic, light sensor and linear potentiometer on the Esplora.
- Esplora Light Calibrator: Check and calibrate the light sensor on the Esplora.
- Esplora Music: Use the Esplora to make some music.
- Esplora Kart: Play the kart racing game using the Esplora as just a controller.
- Esplora Pong: Use Processing to play Pong with Esplora.
- Esplora Remote: Control the outputs by connecting the Esplora to Processing.
- Esplora Tabular: Print the information from its Esplora sensor in a table style.

5.4 Ethernet Library

It is possible to connect to a network (both local and Internet) to use the Arduino Ethernet circuit or shield.

- Advanced Chat Server: Create a straightforward chat server.

- Barometric Pressure HTTP Server: Provides a web page with the readings from the barometric pressure sensor.
- Chat Server: Create a basic chat server.
- DHCP Address Printer: Use DHCP to get an IP address and print it out.
- Dhcp Chat Server: This is a very basic DHCP Chat Server.
- Telnet Client: This is a very basic Telnet client.
- UDP Send/Receive String: Use UDP to receive and send text strings.

5.5 SD Library

Allows you to read and write to SD cards.

- Card Info: Displays information about the SD card.
- Datalogger: Use an SD card to store data from three analog sensors.
- Dump File it Read a document from the Memory card.
- Files: Create and delete a file on an SD card.
- List Files: Print a directory on an SD card's files.
- Read Write: Access data stored on an SD card by reading and writing to it.

5.6 Servo Library

Arduino boards may be used to operate several different servo motors.

- Potentiometer: A potentiometer is used to track the direction of a servo.
- Sweep: A servo motor's shaft is swept back and forth.

5.7 SPI Library

Allows communication using devices that utilize the SPI (Serial Peripheral Interface) bus.

- Barometric Pressure Sensor: Use the SPI protocol to read air temperature and pressure from a sensor.

- Digital Potentiometer Control: Use the SPI protocol to control an AD5206 digital potentiometer.

5.8 Stepper Library

Arduino boards can operate a wide range of stepper motors.

- Motor Knob: A potentiometer is used to control a very precise stepper motor.

- Stepper One Revolution: Rotate the shaft clockwise and counterclockwise one revolution.

- Stepper One Step at a Time: Rotate the shaft one step to ensure the motor is properly wired.

- Stepper Speed Control: A potentiometer is used to control the stepping speed.

Conclusion

This short book, my friends, has already come to an end. Although I hope that Arduino programming will be "off the shelf" in your sector, you will be happy if it only piques your curiosity. This book's ideas are among the most effective approaches for Arduino programmers of all levels to increase their performance and skill. Think about how you and your colleagues will use them and other technologies that will become accessible to increase productivity. This book is for Arduino beginners and experts who wish to learn how to program the board from scratch. The following subject, which is equally significant for beginners and pros, has been tried to be covered in this book.

- Make sure you have the right Arduino hardware and peripherals for your project.
- Connect your Arduino to the Arduino IDE after downloading and installing it.
- Quickly and simply create, develop, upload, and run your first Arduino program.
- Know C grammar, decision-making, strings, data structures, and functions.
- Use pointers to work with memory and avoid common mistakes.
- Add development and testing environments to your Arduino and development and testing shields and functionality electronics.
- Send output and publish input from analog devices or digital interfaces using existing hardware library functions or creating your own
- Put together an Ethernet shield, an Ethernet cable, and a networking application.